Wheels

Written by Frances Ridley

TED SMART

Some wheels are big ...

big wheels

3

... and some wheels are small.

small wheels

Some wheels are fat ...

fat wheels

... and some wheels are thin.

thin wheels

Some wheels are fast ...

fast wheels

... and some wheels are slow.

slow wheels

13

Wheels

big

fat

fast

small

thin

slow

 Ideas for helping your child

Before you start

- Look at the front cover together. What can you see? What do you think the book will be about?

- Read the title. Ask your child to point to the wheels in the picture on the cover. What do wheels do?

- Does it look as if the story will be about real vehicles, or a fiction story?

Help with reading

- Point to the words as you read, to reinforce that we read from left to right. Explain that these words make up the story and tell you what to say.

- Introduce the phrase 'Some wheels are...' and encourage your child to repeat the phrase with you.

- Ask your child what they can see in the pictures. Point to the pictures of new words: big wheels, small wheels, fat wheels, etc, and then find the same details in the bigger pictures on the right.

- The labels repeat the words in the text. Ask your child to match the words in the labels to the words in the text.

- Encourage your child to sound out the first letters of each new word to help them identify it. Praise them every time they get a word right.

Help with discussion

- The story is based on opposites. Talk about other opposites, like hot and cold, and find examples of them.

- Finally, talk about the last double-page of the book. Can your child now read the words for each pair of opposites and remember the order in which they came in the story?

Taking it further

- Look around the house for examples of opposites that appear in the book, e.g. a toy car is slow and a real car is fast, a crayon is small and a table is big.